CAPTIVATING CATS

CAPTIVATING
CATS

Photographs by
RICHARD STACKS
and
RON KIMBALL

Text by
JAMES ARMSTRONG

CEDCO

CEDCO PUBLISHING COMPANY

First Edition

This book published by Cedco Publishing Company, 2955 Kerner Blvd., San Rafael, CA 94901

Printed in Korea

ISBN 1-55912-150-5

CONTENTS

Beware of people who dislike cats.
IRISH PROVERB

A CAT STORY

Anyone who has ever had cats has a story. My favorite story concerns a bright, gold marmalade kitten whose name I never knew because when I met her she hadn't been named yet. Had my situation been different at that time, I could have taken her home and cherished her. But pets at that point in my life simply were not possible, so all I have of her is this indelible memory of a lively little beast who gave me, in a few packed moments, ample proof that she was a special creation; that, in addition to being charming and beautiful, she was possessed of character, personality and intelligence.

It was 20 years ago. A good and magic lady, who it was my good fortune to call a friend, owned a big old rambling place on the outskirts of the little town of Mendocino. The place was more a collection of utilitarian buildings that had grown together over the years than a real house. It sprawled out in an expanse of meadows that fell away to the jig-saw line of high cliffs and sea-stacks that are forever resonant with the pounding of the Pacific's waves. "The Barn," (a misnomer, for there was nothing "barnish" about it) wasn't Suzanne's primary residence. She had arranged for a sculptor and his potter wife to live and have their studios in a part of it, as caretakers. The surrounding meadow was wildly pied with wildflowers in season (especially with swooningly scented bushes of yellow lupin), but it also had a less visible, exploding population of mice and other small varmints. To keep these out of the house, the caretakers kept a small clan of cats.

Where there are cats in the country, there are also bound to be kittens. And thereby hangs my tale:

In a stretch of clean and golden autumn weather, I'd driven up the coast with a friend to spend several days with Suzanne and a couple of her friends. The five of us

Gratitude is the
heart's memory.
FRENCH PROVERB

— all artists of one sort of another — made a grand first evening of it with good food of our own cooking, fine wine from Suzanne's cellar, and much serious talk and even more inspired laughter. Later, by way of settling stomachs and spirits properly, we went for a ramble on the pebbled beach. There was a low tide, and save for the sea sounds and the rhythmic underfoot scrunch of rocks, we walked mainly in silence, savoring all the good things of the night.

Next morning, it wasn't the strong sunlight that woke me, but a distinct sensation of being walked upon. I felt soft, tiny feet against my chest. I opened my eyes just as a small, golden-pink nose, deliciously cool and moist, touched mine. Two sea-green eyes regarded me, and seemed to like what they saw. The kitten gave me a tiny, good-morning kiss with a lick to the end of my nose. I looked toward the door. Sure enough, like many other doors in that rickety old structue, it had come slightly ajar during the night and the latest batch of kittens had wandered in.

"Good morning," I said, and the kitten said something back. I was charmed. Cats that converse with me are the best of cats, I feel (though I've met Siamese who overdo a good thing). I brought up a hand, gave the sleek little head a stroke, and was almost alarmed by the decibel-level purr that cut in with the power of a sports car in passing mode. How can a cat purr that loudly . . . if her purr developed in proportion to her size, by the time she was grown, she'd rattle the houses apart.

I brought both my hands out from under the covers, and there was a lot of petting and scratching and tickling and cuddling, and even more romping and larking-about. She loved the moving-finger-under-the-sheet bit, pouncing and raking with the back feet, and *growling* like the original beast of prey, savage with insensate blood-lust. But, still, never did she really bite or claw. She never got carried away, or went too far in our play. Some kittens, being played with this way, get so excited they require forcible calming. Not this one. She had a sense of proportion, a knowing when enough was enough. I was delighted how she alternated so nicely between

"Devil" and "Darling."

The smell of coffee and toast and convivial sounds from the kitchen downstairs, interrupted our orgy of play and affection. I have yet to encounter a cat or kitten that paid *me* so much attention or was so committed to licking the end of my nose.

"Little Miss Sunshine" or Miss Sunshine, as I came to refer to her, played "pounce-on-the-snake" with my shoelaces, which she relentlessly untied. I was aware that I'd been marked: a certain fur-bearing creature, age perhaps six weeks, regarded me as her personal property. Well, the feeling was mutual.

Whenever I returned from an outing, Miss Sunshine would be waiting. With a sharp little cry of greeting, she'd spring into my lowered arms, scoot up around my shoulders, and, purring like a buzz-saw, begin rubbing her sleek self all around my neck. When I made a lap, she was in it. When I went to bed, she shared it.

On the second evening, I noticed that my new friend had a tiny birth defect. A thin, thread-like membrane ran between the lids of her left eye so she couldn't open it all the way. It seemed to bother her now and again. I'd see her rub the back of a paw across her eyelid, as if trying to clear her vision. Several times, I picked her up and looked at it closely, wondering if perhaps there wasn't something I, or one of the others, could do. But it looked too risky. When I held her and gazed at her eye, wondering what could be done, I marvelled at how she stayed in my hand, staring back at me. I'm sure she understood my care and concern.

As the days galloped by (as good days will), I became more and more concerned about the problem with my small friend's eye. The kitten really belonged to the sculptor's wife. When I asked her about it, she seemed unconcerned. "It'll go away, I suppose" was the best she had to say on the subject. She fed and cared for her cats well enough, but I got a feeling that her concern for them didn't include visits to the local vet.

At last, one evening Suzanne sat me down and said, "Since you're so bothered

That life goes round and round has rather a musical sound.
BOB GRUNDY

To seek takes time like to have a friend takes time.
GEORGIA O'KEEFFE

A dream, I never knew I had, is coming true.
BOB GRUNDY

And 'tis my faith
that every flower
enjoys the air
it breathes.
WORDSWORTH

by this, you're going to have to do something about it yourself. Yes, snipping that little thread of flesh is risky, but if you concentrate on doing it, rather than on the risk, I feel everything will be alright. You have a steady hand and a lot of love. Go ahead."

If she said I could do it, then I could do it. That's how I felt about this wonderful woman, whose mystic quotient affected me powerfully. So one morning after breakfast I hoisted Little Miss Sunshine up onto my lap, laid her on her back in the gully between my legs and took up Suzanne's delicate fingernail scissors. The blades were very thin, and slightly curved. Sunshine lay perfectly still and looked at me, rather than at the scissors. Holding my breath, carefully but quickly, I slipped the delicate instrument into place and snipped.

There was no blood, but it hurt. Miss Sunshine, electrified, emitted an emphatic but not loud cat version of "OW!" and jumped off my lap.

Nobody else made a sound. Fascinated, we watched Miss Sunshine as she turned her back on me and went deliberately toward the door. She stopped suddenly and sat down and seemed to be trying to digest what just happened. Her tail was switching away in an annoyed manner. She shook her head and rubbed her face with her paw. She blinked her eyes as if trying to clear them, tail switching all the time.

And then, damned if she didn't get up, turn around, patter back to me, leap into my lap, and erupt with that racing-car-purr of hers as she stretched up to rub my chin with her nose.

Not many moments of interaction with cats are quite so sharply etched in my memory as that one, and I was amazed to find how deeply my affections had run. When it came time to leave, I felt a profound sadness at leaving behind my little friend.

May you live all the days of your life.
JONATHAN SWIFT

17

It takes a great deal of elevation of thought
to produce a very little elevation of life.
RALPH WALDO EMERSON

The best way out is always through.
ROBERT FROST

What is life but a
series of inspired
follies?
GEORGE BERNARD
SHAW

Tenderness is the
repose of passion.
JOSEPH JOUBERT

SOME MYTHOLOGY AND HISTORY

The Mendocino potter lady and her sculptor husband kept their cats mainly to control vermin, just as people did 7,000 years ago in Jericho, the oldest known city in the world. Dogs were domesticated 40,000 years ago, (the paleontologists tell us), because at that time mankind lived by hunting, and dogs were helpful in bringing down game. It wasn't until men stopped roaming and became farmers, built houses, hearths, and grain silos, and created villages, that cats happened. All that stored grain inevitably attracted rats, who in turn attracted wild cats, which were eventually tamed and — through processes of accidental and intentional breeding and selection that are impossible to reconstruct — developed into the companionate animals we know as house cats.

I cited Jericho, because the cat books I consulted refer to "traces" or "evidences" of cats there 7,000 years ago, but without indicating whether or not they were domesticated. The earliest true records of tame cats are found in tomb paintings of Egypt's 18th dynasty, which began in the 16th century B.C. Paleontologists, archaeologists, and historians seem to agree that the world owes a debt of gratitude to Egypt and its grain warehouses for the domestication of the cat, and that it was from Egypt that cats spread to Europe and Asia. The breeds we know today are apparently descendants of interbreedings of tamed Egyptian cats with other local wildcats . . . of which there are still some 25 species, every one closely resembling a breed of catus.

Though the cat was highly regarded, even treasured, in various cultures from the Near East to Japan and down into Southeast Asia, none of them were ever quite as taken with cats as the ancient Egyptians. From being grateful to the beasts for keeping

Like flowers unfolding, our differences are only various forms of our beauty showing.
BOB GRUNDY

rats out of their grain stores and in the process discovering that they could also be good company around the house, the Egyptians proceeded to the extreme of creating a number of cat-headed goddesses: Basht, Bastet, and Sekhmet were the principal ones plus several other lesser examples, as well. (In one of the books I read on cats, the thesis was offered that our word "puss" or "pussy" may derive — via a not uncommon sound-shift — from various spellings of Basht, or Pasht, a granddaughter of Isis, which puts Basht in the top echelon of the Egyptian pantheon.)

These ancient Egyptians associated the cat with both sun and moon, and one godly puss in particular made sure that the former came up every day. And because this celestial representative of the species was perceived to be so essential to the world's well-being, it is a small wonder that death was the penalty paid by any person so unwise as in any way to bring about the death of one of its mortal kin. When a household's cat died of natural causes, the family went into an elaborate set of mourning rituals, which began with everyone shaving off their eyebrows. Papyri, statues, and carvings on many old walls depict priests praying and making offerings to cats enthroned in splendor, wearing magnificient regalia. Some of these tomb paintings, which are the main source for this information, depict cats doing things that are astonishing. An oft-reproduced fragment of a wall from the tomb of the nobleman Nabmun shows that court official, accompanied by his wife and daughter, out hunting ducks in a stand of papyrus. He's standing on a little reed boat, wild fowl swarming around him, and at his feet is his cat, who has just retrieved a bird with an arrow through it.

Egyptian history is full of cat lore. The Pharaoh Shishak, who sacked Jerusalem and enslaved the Hebrews, was a cat worshipper, and a major Nile Delta city was dedicated to the cat goddess Bubastis. The Greek historian Herodotus, in 450 B.C. was impressed by the temple complex there, which was regarded as a wonder of the world at the time. Indeed, when Bubastis was excavated in the middle of the last

Hopes are but the dreams of those who are awake.
PINDAR

Be good and you will be lonesome.
MARK TWAIN

All mirrors are magical mirrors;
never can we see our faces in them.
LOGAN PEARSALL SMITH

century, arachaeologists marveled not only at the city itself, but at the extent of the catacombs (no pun intended), in which hundreds of thousands of mummified cats were interred each in its little clay sarcophagus. An over-enterprising Victorian businessman thought he saw a red-hot, money-making scheme in this storehouse of dried protein, and shipped 300,000 of these desiccated, linen-wrapped corpses to England. His grisly and insensitive plan was to grind them up and sell the result to farmers as fertilizer. But — quite understandably, I feel — there were few takers, and a lot of these displaced cat cadavers would end up in the basement of the British Museum.

As might be expected, in the good old days the temples of Bubastis swarmed with sacred cats, all lovingly tended by priests and handmaidens. Most wonderful of all, in April and May boatloads of worshippers, sounding cymbals and tooting flutes, barged up the Nile for the big festival there, which was evidently a notably rowdy affair, centering on drinking and what one book I read described as "erotic exhibitionism."

Apparently, this hey-day for cats lasted two or three millennia, during which the export of cats was forbidden. In spite of this, they turned up in Greece at a very early date, and there are records of prized cats being sent as special gifts from pharaohs to other monarchs with whom they had dealings. Very likely, the broader dissemination of cats around the Mediterranean was the work of the Phoenicians, who in all likelihood first discovered the several advantages of having cats as shipmates. They may even have introduced them into Cornwall, where they regularly went to trade for tin. But the Romans were principally responsible for the widest dissemination of cats throughout Europe, for they, too, came to reverence them (though not with the mad abandon of the Egyptians). And if the Phoenicians didn't bring cats to England, the Roman legions certainly did, for a pet cat's skeleton turned up in the ruin of a Roman villa, burned in A.D. 200.

And so, over the centuries, as valued agents of rat control, prized pets, and religious symbols, cats spread down into Africa, up into Europe and Scandinavia, and across the Middle East to China and India. Their inevitable interbreeding with local wildcats gradually gave rise to the different types of cats we know today. Generally speaking, thicker coats evolved naturally in colder climates, while cats nearer the equator kept their short fur.

It is difficult to say exactly what happened to change the cozy, rational relationship that existed between Europeans and cats, but by the Middle Ages, the pendulum had swung the other way. Never mind the good they did in controlling vermin, or any of their other fine qualities. Cats became closely associated with witchcraft and the black arts and they went from being beloved, or at least valued, household companions to become universally regarded as symbols of evil, companions of the devil, and anathema to good Christians.

It is difficult to read accounts of the burnings and impalings and other ghastly things done to cats in Europe for several hundred years. Thousands upon thousands of people were put to death for harboring or even feeding cats. Priests presided over ceremonies in which hundreds of thousands of cats were destroyed. In 1488 Pope Innocent VIII decreed that a witch's cat should be burned with her. As late as the 17th century, just owning a cat could condemn a woman as a witch.

It took the Black Death to save the cat from extinction in Europe. The ships of crusaders returning from the Middle East are blamed for introducing the rats infested with the fleas that carried the deadliest virus man had yet encountered. It was necessary to stop the persecution of cats in order to allow them to control the rats. And so cats survived, but they weren't really accepted as pets until the latter half of the 19th century. At that time, Louis Pasteur discovered the microbe, or germ, and suddenly dogs were considered unhygienic, unlike the "self-cleaning" cat.

By 1860, when the state of Maine held the world's first cat show (honoring the Maine coon cat, which resulted from matings between pet cats and a small wildcat

Nothing in life is to be feared.
It is only to be understood.
MARIE CURIE

Never less alone than when alone.
SAMUEL ROGERS

that became extinct soon after), the tide at last had definitely turned in favor of the cat. Today, there are well over 100 different pedigree breeds standardized and registered in Europe and North America. One of the main problems with cats today is that there are too many of them, so people who don't keep pedigreed cats for breeding are wise to have them spayed or neutered. This doesn't bother the cats in the slightest, and helps control the number of wretched and unwanted kittens that have to be put to sleep, or are left to starve or be run over on the streets, or are checked out to fend for themselves in the country, which they've never been taught to do.

Even with their popularity, however, we're still prey to a small, lingering legacy of cultural conditioning left over from that terrible time during which cats were persecuted. There are still those who consider them to be sly, slinking, stealthy, and untrustworthy, if not actually evil. Many otherwise rational people will tell you, "I simply cannot stand cats; they give me the creeps." (This response has nothing whatsoever to do with allergic reaction, a very real problem.) Unfortunately the superstition about black cats lingers on for some people who find themselves uncomfortable with black cats and many will experience a culturally reflective twinge of alarm when a black cat crosses their path.

There is a budding
morrow in midnight.
JOHN KEATS

Everybody is ignorant, only on different subjects.
WILL ROGERS

Wonders will never cease.
SIR HENRY BATE DUDLEY

I *invent nothing.*
I *rediscover.*
AUGUSTE RODIN

Good taste is the worst vice ever invented.
DAME
EDITH SITWELL

The most I can do for
my friend is simply
to be his friend.
THOREAU

Beauty is its own excuse for being.
RALPH WALDO EMERSON

CAT FACTS, LORE AND MYTH

From the very beginning of their domestication, cats became symbols of motherhood or fecundity. Bastet, Isis, the Greek Demeter and the Celtic Cerridwen were earth goddesses who bestowed (or actually gave birth to) basic grains, and were pictured as cats. The Egyptian Bastet and Greek Artemis were worshipped as virgins. The Norsemen's Freya also had close ties to cats and was pictured riding the heavens in a chariot drawn by three cats.

All of these goddesses were eventually embodied in Mary as the divine Virgin Mother. There is a legend that tells of a cat giving birth to a litter of kittens in the stable where Christ was born. The cat was said to have the marking of a cross on her back.

Roger Carras begins his informative and entertaining book A *Celebration of Cats* with a section devoted to famous haters and lovers of cats. Fascinating reading, and food for thought. I was intrigued to learn that Hitler, Napoleon, and Alexander the Great all hated and feared cats. Alexander was said to pass out cold at the very sight of one.

There is a famous (and probably spurious) anecdote about how, on one of Napoleon's campaigns, a farm cat wandered into his tent and frightened him into an epileptic seizure.

It was good and comforting to know that among the great cat lovers was Abraham Lincoln, and that a long list of my favorite writers and composers and other historical figures also adored cats. However, while I wasn't at all surprised at what I read about Hitler and Napoleon, I chuckled over the news about Alexander the Great. He's my primary hero, and his cat phobia is the first negative thing I've ever

In nature there are neither rewards or punishments —
there are consequences.
ROBERT INGERSOLL

read about him.

When a cat rubs its muzzle against our face, we may think that it's a gesture of great affection, but the truth is that the cat is marking us with a pheronomic secretion from tiny glands near its mouth. When a cat greets you by rubbing itself around your ankles, it is performing a similar "marking" ritual. When it then goes off and licks itself, the cat is sampling indications of where the person previously has been.

Why nine lives? Apparently this is a holdover from the periods when cats had strong religious significance to various cultures. Nine is three threes, a Trinity of Trinities, but Christianity isn't the only religion affected by this mystic number. It would be hard to find a mythology, or a system of witchcraft, in which threes and nines were not focal points of power. The Fates of ancient Greece were three powerful females, as were the Norns, who held the same position in old Norse religion. Cerberus, the guard dog of Hades, has three heads. Christ died in the ninth hour. The River Styx ran nine times around the Greek's hell, Odin gave Freya power over nine worlds. The list runs long through all the old worlds whose psychic remnants still touch us, however peripherally. Macbeth meets three witches on the heath. Most important of all, and perhaps one primal contributor to this body of lore: It takes nine months to make a baby.

Why do cats present us with birds and small animals they have (or have not) killed? Desmond Morris, in his invaluable little book *Cat Watching*, says that it's because they probably view humans as part of their family, most particularly as kittens who need to be taught how to hunt. Which is why, statistically, the biggest bringers-home of these offerings are spayed females: They have no kittens to teach how to hunt, so they redirect this instinct toward us.

Best fishing in troubled waters.
ARISTOTLE

I was born modest; not all over, just in spots.
MARK TWAIN

We carry within us the wonders we seek without us.
SIR THOMAS BROWNE

Silence is one great art of conversation.
WILLIAM HAZLITT

Who are you?
I think I'm me.
Let's compare
and see.
BOB GRUNDY

47

We are each of us angels with only one wing.
And we can only fly embracing each other.
LUCIANO DECRESCENZO

48

There is no reply so sharp as silence.
MONTAIGNE

Philologists tell us that the French, German, Greek, Latin, Russian and Arabic words for cat derive from the Indo-European word *ghad* which means to grasp or catch.

Those darker patches on a Siamese's neck are said to be the fingerprints left by a god who picked up one of them to admire it. And in the old days in Siam, when a member of the royal family died, they were entombed with a live cat. However, there was always a passage through which the cat could emerge. When it did so, it meant that the soul of the deceased had escaped to heaven. The cat was received with great joy and placed in a temple and praised. As recently as 1926, a white Siamese cat occupied a prominent position in a Siamese coronation procession.

In Ghana, some tribes believe that the souls of the dead pass into the bodies of cats.

The Sumatrans used to try to break a drought by tossing a black cat into a river and forcing it to swim ashore pursued by yowling women. The people of Celebes, in the same cause, would tie cats in a sedan chair and carry them around the stricken fields, sloshing water over the cat and imploring the heavens to send rain.

Around 999 A.D., the teen-age Japanese emperor Ichijo became so besotted with a cat and her kittens that he conferred noble status upon them and took up cat breeding. This made cats so fashionable that they were sequestered, and the silk industry — which needed cats to control the mice that ate silkworm cocoons — nearly went out of business. Also the stores of rice were threatened under the same circumstances. Even so, it was a long time before a subsequent emperor decreed that cats be free and anyone could own one.

I am a deeply superficial person.
ANDY WARHOL

Only Australia and Antarctica never had wild cats. The other five continents have known them for forty million years.

Man is the only animal known to keep pets. However, quite recently, a female gorilla named Koko, who had been taught to communicate with sign language, became much attached to a kitten. When the kitten was accidentally killed, KoKo grieved so that a substitute had to be quickly found. KoKo accepted the new kitten with joy, and all on her own, named it after the first one.

It is true — I've always loved.
ALICE WALKER

When it is dark enough, you can see the stars.
CHARLES A. BEARD

Only the loving find love, and
they never have to seek for it.
D.H. LAWRENCE

The happiest of all lives
is a busy solitude.
VOLTAIRE

To be loved, be loveable.
OVID

He makes no friend who never made a foe.
TENNYSON

We are the music-makers, and we are
the dreamers of dreams.
ARTHUR WILLIAM O'SHAUGHNESSY

I *think,*
therefore I *am.*
DESCARTES

A CAT CALLED YOO-HOO

Yellowing snapshots in the ratty old family picture albums amply demonstrate that there were always cats in the Armstrong family, but the first one I really remember was the white short-hair with one blue eye and one green one. To the best of my recollection, he never had an official name beyond "White Kitty," but what he responded to was "Yoo-Hoo!", which was how mother summoned him to his supper. Mother fancied herself a bit of a character (always respectable, but still a character), and it was her practice to stand out on the back steps and hoot "Yoo-Hoo!" until White Kitty came scooting under the hedge and gave her ankle a rub on his way into the kitchen.

Mother had a trained voice of considerable power (she could, and always did, hit that optional high note at the end of "The Star Spangled Banner") and these backyard utterances, though always perfectly mellifluous, often scratched the nerves of the neighbor ladies. Many a day, first one and then another, and then as many as eight of them would be moved to fling up a window or step onto a porch and respond in kind. On such occasions, our part of the neighborhood would ring with overlapping yoo-hoos, 'til it sounded like a convention of yodelers trying out echoes in the Alps.

A privacy of glorious light is thin.
WORDSWORTH

How beautiful it is to do nothing, then rest afterward.
SPANISH PROVERB

62

We're all in this together — by ourselves.
LILY TOMLIN

I *love those who long for the impossible.*
GOETHE

64

My belief is
that to have
no wants is
devine.
SOCRATES

GUNTHER THE BUTLER CAT

Once when I lived in Hollywood and tried to break into writing for movies and television, I shared an enormous old house with four other gentlemen. This was in the mid-Sixties, when a three-story house with four residential suites, the usual reception rooms, servants' quarters, butler's pantry, library, a half-acre of lawn, a 60-foot pool and some tennis courts in a decent part of town could be rented for $625 a month.

One of the most valued members of the household was Tom's cat, Gunther. Gunther was about five years old, an immense, portly, medium long-haired brown tabby cat gifted with tremendous presence and even more charm, who always moved slowly and deliberately. Oh, if he were unduly startled, he could scamper and scoot with the best, but he resented it, and whoever or whatever might cause him thus to depart from his preferred dignity of demeanor would come in for some truly filthy looks.

Gunther was by nature a greeter. When he'd see you down the hall, out in the yard, across a crowded room, he'd change course and, with his own highly distinctive brand of dignity, move toward you as though he was a small fuzzy cloud being wafted along by a gentle breeze that touched him alone. He'd give your ankles a rub, and then stand there, vast plume of tail languidly erect and gently waving at the tip, looking up into your face, waiting for a pet. Occasionally, he would pass a comment, on the weather perhaps, or how happy he was to see you. As I said, Gunther had charm.

He was truly a great cat, and — watching him meet his guests in the entrance hall, or circulate at a party — I was, time and again, reminded of Beach, the ineffably imperturable, archetypical English butler who graces all the hilarious P.G. Wodehouse novels centering in Blandings Castle. And I'd think to myself that if the Darling family

Character is destiny.
HERACLITUS

Give me freedom, give me the sky.
BOB GRUNDY

The great pleasure in life
is doing what people say
you cannot do.
WALTER BAGEHOT

(in "Peter Pan") could have a St. Bernard as nanny, why couldn't this household have a cat — Gunther — as butler?

One evening, when all the house's residents were present at the same time, we decided to collaborate on an impromptu supper, which — the day being warm — we ate on the iron-work dining-set out on the loggia. That was the evening Tom told us how he'd happened to acquire Gunther.

Supper was over and conversation had died down. George motioned with his head, directing our attention to the other end of the lawn where Gunther was stalking one of the resident robins, out for a bedtime worm. Knowing Gunther, we recognized this as a put on performance because he knew that he was being observed and that bird-stalking was expected of self-respecting cats as part of their backyard duty. He was pleased to entertain us this way, but only as long as we didn't expect him actually to catch or (God forbid!) eat one. Besides, his dignity was dear to him, and he was too portly to be either dignified or effective in the final dash. The robin knew he was there, and evidently also knew Gunther, for he ignored him and hopped about perkily behind his russet spinnaker of a chest, cocking his dark head this way and that, listening for whatever racket it is that worms make digesting the dirt under our lawns. (I myself have always imagined it as a raspy, intermittent humming sound.) Hearing one, he turned one ear downwards, pecked, turned the other ear, pecked again. Gunther relaxed from his stalker's crouch into a lying down position, and watched placidly while the bird — with occasional backward glances at the tabby-striped, Persian-furred sphinx lying not 20 feet behind him — pecked and tugged and finally hauled up a fat wriggle of worm. When he'd gulped it down, Gunther rose politely, ready to continue. But an imperative squawk from a nearby tree summoned the robin, and with a flit and a flutter, he was gone. Gunther observed his line of flight, and then sat down to deliver himself of one of those enormous cat yawns that seem to turn their heads inside out. Then with deliberate slowness he ambled over, his mighty plume

*Comedy is simply
a funny way of
being serious.*
PETER USTINOV

You can only apologize for so much.
STEVEN STILLS

Chaos is come again.
WILLIAM SHAKESPEARE

of tail straight up and undulating majestically, to rub his way around our legs, purring like a fuzzy rock tumbler, and accepting our attentions with squinch-eyed delight.

Tom hoisted him onto his lap and disposed him there, back down, head hanging, in one of his favorite positions. "Did I ever tell you how I came to acquire this beast?" he asked, his voice full of affection. We shook our heads. "It was a typical performance, absolutely typical." He fluffed the floss on Gunther's tummy, and Gunther curled his paws in. "You do appreciate, don't you, that this really is the world's weirdest cat?" We all understood that by "weird" he meant "wonderful, marvelous, adorable, magical, irreplaceable," and we smiled and nodded.

"Well, four years back, I was in the market for a kitten. So I take myself off to the SPCA and let the nice ladies bring out boxes of kittens for me to choose from. And all the time I'm looking the little darlings over, there's this half-grown cat mooching around checking me out. First, he just stands a little ways off with his tail up, looking, but after he's made up his mind (and I could see him *making up his mind*, let me tell you), he sashays over and stands by me and looks me up and down. I mean, he's really *inspecting* me. So I reach down and give him a pet and a tickle behind the ears and he likes it. He walks off and sits down again a few feet away, and I notice he seems to be *thinking* about something. Well, this performance strikes me as pretty remarkable, but it's a kitten I'm there for, so I turn away. And then, damned if he doesn't come back and sit himself right down on my foot and look up at me as though he's telling me something. But I'm still thinking kitten, so I don't get the message. So I move the foot and he has to get off. Which he does and wanders off and I forget about him because one of the SPCA ladies brings me another litter of adorable short-hair kitties, all black, with white noses and feet and ears and tail-tips. You know the kind."

"Jellicoe cats, they're called," I said.

"Really? I never knew that. Anyhow, I take out one that appeals to me and squat

Wherever we go — there we are.
BOB GRUNDY

down to play around and generally get acquainted. And then, damned if this half-grown character with the long fur doesn't walk up, as purposefully as you please, take the darling kitten right out of my hands and carry it over and dump it back in the box with its brothers and sisters. Then he comes back, sits on my foot again, looks up into my face and says, '*Meow!*' . . . what could I do? I'd been *picked!* So we went home together and lived happily ever after." He gave Gunther's tummy fur another fluff, then let him slide off his lap. "I know something special when it hits me over the head, believe me."

In the eyes, cats to inspire — the longing of affections desire.
M.K. SMITH

If music be the food of love, play on.
WILLIAM SHAKESPEARE

*Nature never did
betray the heart
that loved her.*
WORDSWORTH

Nothing is black or white but shades of grey.
R.C. YOUNG

Nothing is so sweet as anticipation.
M.K. SMITH

Maybe we secretly envy cats.
BARBARA WEBSTER

Home is the place where,
when you have to go there,
they have to take you in.
ROBERT FROST

God Almighty hates a quitter.
GEN. SAMUEL FESSENDEN

*Am I my
brother's keeper?*
OLD TESTAMENT

The rest is silence.

WILLIAM SHAKESPEARE

BIBLIOGRAPHY

The Velvet Paw, by Jean Conger
    Obolensky, Inc., NY, 1963

A Celebration of Cats, by Roger A. Caras
    Simon & Schuster, NY, 1986

The Complete Cat Encyclopedia, ed. Grace Pond
    Crown, NY, 1972

Cats: A Celebration, by Elizabeth Hamilton
    Scribner's, NY, 1979

*Cat Watching, (Why cats purr and everything else
  you ever wanted to know,)* by Desmons Morriss
    Crown, NY, 1986

The Complete Cat Encyclopedia, edited by Grace Pond
    Crown, NY, 1972